W9-BHI-720

Animal Rescue

Sally Morgan

Cherrytree Books are distributed in the United States
by Black Rabbit Books, P.O. Box 3263, Mankato, MN 56002

U.S. publication copyright © Cherrytree Books 2010
International copyright reserved in all countries.
No part of this book may be reproduced in any form without
written permission from the publishers.

Printed in China.

Library of Congress Cataloging-in-Publication Data

Morgan, Sally.
  Animal rescue / Sally Morgan.
      p. cm. -- (Helping our planet)
  Includes index.
  ISBN 978-1-84234-606-8 (library bound)
  1. Animal rescue--Juvenile literature. 2. Wildlife rescue--Juvenile literature.
  3. Wildlife conservation--Juvenile literature. 4. Endangered species--Juvenile literature.
I. Title. II. Series.

  QL83.M6645 2011
  333.95'416--dc22

2010000035

First Edition
9 8 7 6 5 4 3 2 1

First published in 2009 by Evans Brothers Ltd.
2A Portman Mansions, Chiltern Street, London W1U 6NR, United Kingdom

Copyright © Evans Brothers Ltd. 2009

Picture Credits:
Cover: main image Reinhard Dirscherl; inset, left to to right: Robert Pickett, Robert Baldwin, Brian
Cushing; title page Michael Gore; p6 Fritz Polking; p7 Phillip Colla; p8 Robert Pickett; p9 Fritz Polking;
p10 Erik Schaffer; p11 Fritz Polking; p12 Peter Cairns; p13 Ian Harwood; p14 Reinhard Dirscherl; p15
Luc Hosten; p16 Robert Baldwin; p17 Quentin Bates; p18 Michael Gore; p19 Mike Whittle; p20 Stephen
Coyne; p21 Wayne Lawler; p22 Michael Gore; p23 Satyendra Tiwari; p24 Mike Maidment; p25 Brian
Cushing; p26 Robert Pickett; p27 Reinhard Dirscherl

Printed on chlorine free paper from sustainably managed sources.

Contents

Animals In Danger

Imagine a world without tigers, polar bears, giant pandas, or whales in the sea. It seems impossible but one day these animals and many others may disappear forever and become extinct. Every 20 minutes, a type of animal or plant becomes extinct. That's more than 70 every day.

▼ Giant pandas are under threat because the bamboo forests where they live have been cleared.

In some parts of the world, whales are still hunted for their meat. They are also threatened by pollution and oil spills.

Animals are in danger. The places where they live, their habitats, are disappearing. Some animals are hunted by people for their fur, horns, or bones, while too many fish are taken from the sea for food. Many animals are harmed by pollution. Pollution makes the air, sea, or land dirty and unsafe.

Find Out More

What is your favorite animal? Do you know where it lives or what it eats? Learn more about this animal on the Internet. Go to http://www.globio.org.

Amazing Animals

There are millions of different types of animals in the world, and each has an important job to do. For example, butterflies, bees, and other insects help plants to produce seeds, while other animals such as birds and monkeys help to scatter seeds.

Butterflies help flowers to make seeds. They carry pollen from one flower to another.

Find Out More

Animals come in all shapes and sizes, but they are all adapted to the environment in which they live. Find out more about all the amazing animals in the world by visiting http://kids.nationalgeographic.com/Animals/.

In a food chain, plants are eaten by herbivores (plant-eating animals) and herbivores are eaten by carnivores (meat-eating animals). If one type of herbivore or carnivore disappears, the food chain is broken. When this happens, some animals may starve and die.

Giraffes and zebras are herbivores. They are hunted by carnivores such as lions.

Burning Rain Forests

Rain forests are thick forests that are found in the warm, wet parts of the world, such as Brazil, Central Africa, and Southeast Asia. They are home to about half of all the different types of animals that live on Earth. But the rain forests are disappearing fast. The trees are cut down and the wood is used for building.

▼ Forests are burned down to make space to grow crops, graze cattle, and build new homes.

In many places forests are cleared without permission. Now, some of the most important rain forests are protected and their animals are safe.

What Can Be Done?

Conservation groups and charities can collect money and use it to buy areas of rain forests. Then they can look after their part of a rain forest and protect the animals that live in it.

The hyacinth macaw is a type of parrot. Many of these birds have lost their homes in the wild and they are now at risk of becoming extinct.

Digging Up Homes

Every day more people are born in the world and they, like everyone else, need food. Large areas of grassland have been plowed up to make way for fields of food crops. Wheat and corn now grow in places where animals used to graze.

You Choose

Which do you think is more important, food and homes for people or food and homes for animals?

Farmers wanted to grow wheat on the grasslands where bison like these lived. Now the bison live in protected areas.

Towns and cities are getting larger. New homes, roads, schools, and factories are built on land that was once home to animals.

When people clear land to build new homes for themselves, homes for animals may be lost.

At Risk In the Oceans

The vast oceans are home to many different animals, from huge blue whales to tiny plankton. The oceans are at risk, especially the shallow areas along coasts.

Coral reefs are beautiful underwater homes to fish, shrimp, sea anemones, and many other animals. They can be harmed by people and pollution.

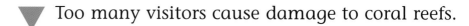
Too many visitors cause damage to coral reefs.

People dump trash and other wastes in the oceans. Animals get tangled up in plastic bags or poisoned by the waste.

What Can Be Done?

Around the world, thousands of volunteers clear trash from beaches while divers collect trash underwater. This stops animals from becoming trapped and harmed by the trash.

▼ This gannet, a type of seabird, died when plastic netting became twisted around its beak.

Fishing Dangers

People have fished the oceans for thousands of years, but the numbers of fish are falling fast. Modern fishing boats have huge nets which catch thousands of fish in one go.

It's not just fish that are caught. The nets trap other animals such as dolphins, whales, and turtles. Now there are new designs of nets that allow these larger animals to escape.

 A diver frees a turtle caught in a net.

Some countries have laws that control the number of fish that are caught and in some places fishing is banned.

You Choose

The Atlantic cod is at risk of becoming extinct. However, people still catch and eat it. Do you think it is right to eat an animal that is at risk? What could people do instead?

This fishing boat has caught many different types of fish from the seabed.

Captured!

Lizards, monkeys, and brightly colored birds make unusual pets. Sadly, many of these animals are trapped, taken from the wild and sold around the world. Many die before they reach a pet store.

These monkeys are for sale in a market in Indonesia.

Find Out More

There are laws to stop the trade in rare animals, and special police who are trained to stop this crime. Find out more about wildlife crime at http://www.traffic.org.

People do not only take animals from the wild to sell as pets. Animal thieves, called poachers, capture some animals. Then they kill them and sell their skin, bones, teeth, or meat.

▼ Experts think that, in the last 100 years, the number of tigers left in the wild has fallen by 95 percent.

Vacation Souvenirs

Have you ever hunted for shells on a beach?
The shells are empty because the animal has died. However, in some places people collect living animals and kill them to get their shell. Coral is collected and made into jewelry. The shells and coral are sold as souvenirs to tourists.

You choose

If you saw some brightly colored shells, a beautiful butterfly or pieces of coral for sale in a shop, would you be tempted to buy them?

Many tropical butterflies have dazzling wings and people like to collect them. They kill the butterflies and display them pinned to a board.

This man is selling butterflies in a market.

Find Out More

It is illegal to bring home many souvenirs such as conch shells, coral, ivory, tortoiseshell, shark teeth, snake, and lizard skin. Find out which souvenirs are illegal. Go to http://www.responsibletravel.org/home/index.html.

Protect Their Homes!

We can protect animal habitats. We can make huge parks and reserves where the animals are safe and people can visit them. Hunters and loggers cannot harm the plants and animals.

Protecting the oceans is just as important. Marine national parks protect coral reefs and have areas where fish can breed in safety.

The Antarctic is a World Park which is home to millions of penguins and seals.

What Can Be Done?

Wildlife vacations are very popular. Tourists and their local guides take care to protect the habitats they visit for the animals that live there.

Rescue Centers

The people who work in animal rescue centers have an important job. They take in animals that have been harmed or treated cruelly. They look after them until they are ready to return to the wild.

People can help animals that are in danger of becoming extinct. They can give them a home where the animals are safe and they can breed.

People have saved the Przewalski's horse from becoming extinct.

The snow leopard is an endangered animal. People have passed laws to protect it, so that it will not become extinct.

You Choose

There are many zoos around the world where people can see animals up close. Do you think it is right for animals to be kept in zoos?

Find Out More

Modern zoos look after many endangered animals — for example, the giant panda. You can watch the webcam in the giant panda enclosure at the National Zoological Park Washington, DC. Go to http://nationalzoo.si.edu/Animals/GiantPandas/.

Back To the Wild

Sometimes people from zoos and rescue centers can release animals back into the wild. In South America for example, the golden lion tamarin, a type of monkey, has been released back into the rain forest. Now tamarins have increased in number and their future is safe.

▼ A golden lion tamarin

Sometimes people rescue animals from oil spills or burning rain forests, or from being sold in pet stores. They aim to release these animals back to their homes in the wild. For example, people can take rescued orangutans to special reserves where they teach them how to live in the rain forest.

This orangutan was rescued as a youngster and is having fun in the rain forest.

What Can Be Done?

Conservation groups and charities need money to fund their projects. See if you can raise money at school to help people protect a particular animal.

Glossary

adapted suited, become used to

carnivore an animal that eats other animals

conservation protection or preservation of an animal, plant or habitat

endangered at risk of becoming extinct

extinct no longer living

food chain the series of links that connects plants, herbivores, and carnivores in a habitat

graze to eat the grass growing on an area of land

habitat the place where an animal or a plant lives

herbivore an animal that eats plants

illegal against the law

loggers people who cut down trees and sell the wood

marine to do with the oceans

national park a protected area in a country that people can visit where animals and plants are kept safe

plowed soil that has been turned over ready to plant crops

pollution harm to the environment by substances that have been released into the air, water, or onto the land

rain forest dense tropical forest

volunteer a helper, someone who is working without being paid

Index

Numbers in **bold** refer to pictures.